Robert Quackenbush

HERE A PLANT, THERE A PLANT, EVERYWHERE A PLANT, PLANT!

A STORY OF LUTHER BURBANK

Luther Burbank Home & Gardens
SANTA ROSA, CALIFORNIA

Luther Burbank Home & Gardens

CITY OF

Santa Rosa

**Here A Plant, There A Plant, Everywhere A Plant, Plant!
A Story of Luther Burbank**

New Edition

Published in 1995
Second printing 1999

Luther Burbank Home & Gardens
City of Santa Rosa
P.O. Box 1678
Santa Rosa, CA 95402

Library of Congress Catalog Card Number: 94-73390

ISBN: 0-9637883-1-0

Luther Burbank Home & Gardens is grateful for
partial funding of this new edition by the
Sonoma County Community Foundation

Printed in the United States of America
by Penny Wise Printing

Luther Burbank, the thirteenth of fifteen children, was born on March 7, 1849, in Lancaster, Massachusetts. He grew up on a farm knowing mud pies, grasshoppers, water bugs, tadpoles, mud turtles, trees to climb, brooks to wade in, rocks to roll, woodchucks, bats, bees, butterflies, sand snakes, and hornets. But he loved plants most of all. Even a potted cactus gave him more pleasure than any toy. He got this love of plants from his mother, who had a wonderful garden and an unusual talent for making things grow.

At the age of twenty-one, Burbank completed his education at Lancaster Academy. Soon after that, his father died. With his small inheritance, Luther bought land. He had already decided to make plant-breeding his lifework. To earn money he had a truck garden, producing vegetables for sale at the market in a nearby town. But in his free hours, he experimented with creating better vegetables. He would save the seeds from only his sturdiest and best plants. Then he would nurture these superior varieties through several generations until he created the better breeds. He especially wanted to create a better potato. He knew there was great demand for a whiter, larger potato to replace the undersized reddish variety. Then one day he had an amazing stroke of good fortune. Burbank discovered a rare seed-ball with twenty-three seeds ripening on one of his Early Rose potato plants. He knew that from these seeds he could grow seedlings—one of which might possibly turn up the potato he was seeking. A playful dog nearly got away with the prize, but Burbank got it back.

Burbank carefully tended and planted the seeds, which produced twenty-three healthy seedlings. As they grew, two of the plants produced larger, whiter, and sweeter potatoes than Burbank had ever seen before. The next year he planted the potatoes from these two plants, and they in turn produced even larger potatoes than any yet grown. The chance seed-ball had given the world the Burbank Potato, which today yields millions of dollars every year to its growers. But Burbank sold his prize new variety to a seedsman for only one hundred and fifty dollars! However, this was just enough money for what Burbank had in mind—a railroad ticket to California. He packed his suitcase with a few clothes and ten of his potatoes that he had been allowed to keep. The warmer western climate where he could grow things all year round was where he wanted to be.

Burbank was overjoyed when he arrived in Santa Rosa, California, in 1875. It was all he dreamed it would be, and more. He wrote home about the wonders to be found there—cabbages as big as washtubs, squash three feet long, and grapes so plentiful that they were used for hog feed. Burbank was known for his habit of telling tall stories, and his family and friends knew better than to believe everything he said. But one thing is clear: Burbank was enthusiastic about California. And he was willing to do any kind of job, like cleaning chicken coops, so he could stay. In between odd jobs, he raised plants on small plots of land that he bought with money he saved.

Burbank's first big order came in 1881 from Mr. Warren Dutton, a prosperous merchant who wanted twenty thousand prune trees ready to set out by that coming fall. It was an impossible task, because prune seedlings grow very slowly and it was already March. They could never be ready in time. But Burbank figured it might be done if prune buds were grafted—or "June budded"—into almond seedlings. He believed that the almond seedlings, being rapid growers, would force early budding of the prune buds. He set to work.

By June, Burbank had grown twenty thousand almond seedlings. He began to graft the prune buds to the seedlings. He sliced an opening in each almond stock and inserted a prune bud. After a few days, when the buds had made good unions with the stocks, the tops of the almond seedlings were broken above the prune buds and left hanging so the prune buds would be forced to grow. Miraculously, the buds burst and grew into seedlings. And by December, Burbank delivered the young prune trees to the satisfied—and surprised—customer.

With the success of the prune trees, Burbank's small nursery began attracting crowds of would-be buyers of his plants and seeds. He kept increasing the size of his nursery with the profits. By 1884 he had four acres of land in Santa Rosa and a house surrounded by a greenhouse, barns, gardens and trees. Here he carried out more than a hundred thousand experiments, involving six thousand different kinds of plants.

Many of the experiments were designed to create better plants by cultivating only the best variety of each generation, as he had done to create the Burbank Potato. This is called line breeding. In addition, he created new plants by mixing the pollen of one plant with the pollen of another. Plants are often crossbred accidentally in nature by pollen-carrying birds and insects or by the wind. But Burbank did crossbreeding— or hybridization—by hand. He carefully chose the plants to be crossed, hoping for a new plant that would have the best qualities of both parent plants.

His experiments took so much space that he sometimes grafted a hundred different varieties on a single tree. That way he could produce fruits sooner and compare their qualities more easily.

Burbank's typical day began at five o'clock in the morning. He would go out into the hills of Santa Rosa looking for new and unusual plants. If he saw a particularly interesting one, he marked it with a piece of cloth so he could come back to gather its seeds when they were ripe. Sometimes he ran out of cloth and was forced to tear up his handkerchief or necktie, or even pull a shoelace from his shoe. More than once he came flopping back to the nursery minus his shoelaces and parts of his clothing. Then he would go out and walk through the gardens surrounding his house to select the plants he wanted to keep for a particular variety he was seeking. The hundreds of rejected plants he would haul to a hillside and burn. As neighbors watched the giant bonfires, they wondered about the sanity of a man who seemed to grow things just to destroy them. This would go on until dark, and then Burbank would have an early supper and go to bed to be ready for another busy day.

By 1885 Burbank was well established in the nursery business. To his nursery he added a farm of eighteen acres at Sebastopol, California, where he raised his seeds and offered them for sale in England, Europe, the Orient, and Australia. As Burbank's experimental work became known outside Santa Rosa Valley, letters and seeds came pouring in. Enthusiastic fans sent him corn kernels from the grave of a Zulu king in Africa, seeds from the ruins of the cliff dwellers in the Grand Canyon, and even rock melon and cantaloupe seeds from New Guinea. Burbank made use of them all by crossing them with California flowers and fruits to see what he could achieve. One of these was a special plum.

Burbank had read a sailor's account of a luscious Japanese plum with juicy red meat. He dreamed of introducing it to American fruit growers. But this plum tree would not survive in many of America's climates and soils. So when he received twelve varieties of plum seedlings from Japan, he crossbred them with the sturdier but poorer-fruiting American and European varieties. After several generations and thousands of crossings, he produced some of the finest plums ever known.

21

In 1888 Burbank sold part of his nursery business. He announced that in the future he would work almost exclusively toward developing new and unusual plants. Then he took a long-needed vacation in Massachusetts. On his return trip to California, he became acquainted with a woman named Helen A. Coleman. Two years later they were married. But the marriage did not last. Burbank's wife yelled at him, nagged him, threatened to shoot him, bedeviled him, blackened both of his eyes, and forced him to live in the barn. Finally, after six years of this, Burbank got a divorce. And it was a long time—over twenty years—before he ever thought of getting married again.

NEW CREATIONS IN FRUITS AND FLOWERS

During this stressful time, Burbank was able to put together a catalog of his best crossbred plant varieties. Issued in June 1893, the fifty-two page brochure was entitled "New Creations in Fruits and Flowers." It was a cornucopia of new berries, plums, and prunes, five new seedling roses, a new poppy named "Silver Lining," and even a white blackberry. Some of his experiments were also listed. They included crosses of peaches with almonds, plums with apricots, quinces with apples, and potatoes with tomatoes. Although some of these unusual crosses never produced marketable fruits and vegetables (particularly the potato and tomato combination), they were valuable as research for other experimenters. To Burbank's surprise, the catalog created a sensation, and he became internationally famous overnight.

There were all kinds of reactions to Burbank's catalog, and not all of them were good. Storms of protest came from some religious and civic groups who thought no man could or should have the power of creation. Even so, within a year of the catalog's publication all the plants and seeds listed in it were sold. Every year after that, Burbank's sales kept growing. In 1897 his gross sales exceeded $16,000. And by the time he was fifty, Burbank found himself firmly established in the public eye as "The Wizard of Horticulture" and "The Edison of Horticultural Mysteries."

Burbank's largest single sale of $26,000 (worth many times that amount in today's money) was for the result of one of his most amazing experiments. It was the removal of spines from desert cactus to make edible fodder for cattle. The work required breeding and crossbreeding hundreds of cactus varieties over a period of twenty years until a spineless variety evolved. But more than that, Burbank's final result was a spineless cactus that also bore fruit!

What Burbank liked most about his fame were the friendships he made with other famous people the world over, including Henry Ford and Thomas Edison. But what he didn't like about it was the crowd of reporters who were always around his home. They camped on his doorstep from before breakfast until as late as midnight, reporting and exaggerating everything he did. Worst of all were the newspaper reports about his farm during the San Francisco earthquake of 1906, which also affected Santa Rosa. Burbank's greenhouse and plants escaped damage, but his house—just a few feet away—suffered severe cracks during the quake and a chimney was knocked down. Much to Burbank's dismay, the reporters made it sound as if supernatural powers had protected his work.

Even with his fame and success, Burbank often had trouble finding money to keep up with his experiments. Then, in 1905, the Carnegie Institute in Washington, D.C., awarded him a grant. The Institute was to pay him $10,000 a year for ten years; he, in turn, would keep accurate records of his experiments to pass on through history. Along with the grant came an expert to help Burbank write everything down. But the Institute could not accept Burbank's unique, unscientific method of record-keeping. In addition, Burbank did not like taking time from his experiments to answer questions. Before long the grant was cancelled, and Burbank spent his remaining years at work on his own, just as before. Except that years later—when he was 67—he did acquire a partner. A new wife! Elizabeth Waters was forty years younger than Burbank. But that didn't make any difference to him, because she never, never yelled at him or blackened his eyes. So Burbank spent the remainder of his years quite content.

Epilogue

Luther Burbank contributed much to the wealth and good eating of the nation and the world. But during his lifetime he was a controversial figure, and his scientific work was denounced in newspapers and from pulpits. It was mainly his work in crossbreeding that upset people. Most plant-breeders of that time considered it somehow improper to cross, for example, an apple with a blackberry. But Luther Burbank made the attempt as naturally as he would reach down to pick a flower. In spite of criticism, the public took Burbank to its heart, and fame and honors were showered on him.

There is no doubt that for his plums and potatoes alone, Burbank must be ranked among the most successful breeders in horticultural history. Beside them is placed the Shasta Daisy, his most successful flower. Other successes have been lost with time. That's because tastes change, and breeders are always at work trying to produce something better. Few new creations remain in seed catalogs for more than five or ten years. So of the more than eight hundred fruits and flowers that Burbank improved, only a few remain. Still, he has had no equals, and his plants are the ancestors of many of today's vegetables and flowers. For this reason, his work is immortal.

About the Author

ROBERT QUACKENBUSH is a popular author/artist of over one hundred and sixty books for young readers, including a number of biographies. His books are notable for the wit, humorous cartoon illustrations, and lively story lines that have become Robert Quackenbush's own special trademark. His story of Luther Burbank was inspired by childhood memories of his mother and grandmother, who were gardening enthusiasts, telling him about Luther Burbank and his remarkable work. He incorporated into the book some of the jokes that have become associated with Luther Burbank and his legendary crossbreeding experiments. They were told to him by children he met during his author tours to schools and libraries in the U. S. (including Alaska), South America and the Middle East. Born in California and reared in Arizona, Robert Quackenbush now lives in New York City with his wife, Margie, and their son, Piet, to whom this book is dedicated. His art has been exhibited in leading museums, including the Whitney and the Smithsonian Institution. He is a three-time winner of the American Flag Institute Award for his outstanding contributions to the field of children's literature, as well as being a winner of an Edgar Allen Poe Special Award for best juvenile mystery. In addition to his books, he teaches art to children and adults at his studio.